Seek & Speak
SPANISH Words

Louise Millar

Illustrations by Louise Comfort
Spanish adviser: Diego Blasco Vázquez
Spanish advisor, Happy Fox edition: Rosi Perea

Happy Fox
BOOKS

En la granja

Look for these words in the big picture.

el caballo
el kah-BAH-yoh
horse

la vaca
lah BAH-kah
cow

el perro
el PEH-roh
dog

Can you find another cat somewhere in the book?

el ratón
el rah-TOHN
mouse

2

On the farm

el cerdo
el SEHR-doh
pig

la oveja
lah oh-BEH-hah
sheep

el pato
el PAH-toh
duck

la cabra
lah KAH-brah
goat

el gato
el GAH-toh
cat

Say the Spanish word aloud.

En clase

Look for these words in the big picture.

la profesora
lah proh-feh-SOHR-ah
teacher

la silla
lah SEE-yah
chair

la mesa
lah MEH-sah
table

el lápiz de color
el LAH-pees deh koh-LOHR
colored pencil

Find another chair somewhere in the book.

4

In the classroom

el libro
el LEE-broh
book

el pegamento
el peh-gah-MEHN-toh
glue

la computadora
lah kohm-poo-tah-DOH-rah
computer

Say the Spanish word aloud.

la pluma
lah PLOO-mah
pen

el papel
el pah-PEHL
paper

5

El cuerpo

Look for these words in the big picture.

la cabeza
lah kah-BEH-sah
head

los ojos
lohs OH-hohs
eyes

la nariz
la nah-REES
nose

la boca
lah BOH-kah
mouth

Count the number of children at the party.

6

Your body

la mano
lah MAH-noh
hand

la pierna
lah PYEHR-nah
leg

el pie
el PYEH
foot

los hombros
lohs OHM-brohs
shoulders

Say the Spanish word aloud.

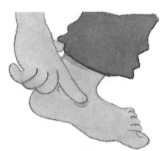

el brazo
el BRAH-soh
arm

Los colores en la selva

Look for these words in the big picture.

rojo/a
RROH-hoh/hah
red

azul
ah-SOOL
blue

How many purple things are in the scene?

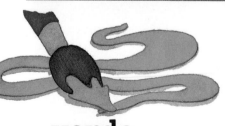

verde
BEHR-deh
green

amarillo/a
ah-mah-REE-yoh/yah
yellow

Colors in the jungle

blanco/a
BLAHN-koh/kah
white

morado/a
moh-RAH-doh/dah
purple

marrón
mah-RROHN
brown

Say the Spanish word aloud.

naranja
nah-RAHN-hah
orange

negro/a
NEH-groh/grah
black

El baúl de los disfraces

Look for these words in the big picture.

la falda
FAHL-dah
skirt

el vestido
el behs-TEE-doh
dress

Find someone on another page wearing a hat.

los zapatos
lohs sah-PAH-tohs
shoes

Say the Spanish word aloud.

The dressing-up box

el pantalón

el pahn-tah-LOHN
pants

la camisa

lah kah-MEE-sah
shirt

el abrigo

el ah-BREE-goh
coat

los calcetines

lohs kahl-sehn-TEE-nehs
socks

el sombrero

el sohm-BREH-roh
hat

el pijama

el pee-HAH-mah
pajamas

11

En el zoológico

la jirafa
lah hee-RAH-fah
giraffe

el león
el leh-OHN
lion

el tigre
el TEE-greh
tiger

el cocodrilo
el koh-koh-DREE-loh
crocodile

At the zoo

el elefante
el eh-leh-FAHN-teh
elephant

el oso polar
el OH-soh poh-LAHR
polar bear

el hipopótamo
el ee-poh-POH-tah-moh
hippopotamus

la víbora
lah BEE-boh-rah
snake

Say the Spanish word aloud.

el delfín
el dehl-FEEN
dolphin

El transporte

Look for these words in the big picture.

el autobús
el ow-toh-BOOS
bus

la parada
lah pah-RAH-dah
bus stop

la acera
lah ah-SEH-rah
sidewalk

Find a car somewhere else in the book.

la calle
lah KAH-yeh
street

Transportation

el semáforo
el seh-MAH-foh-roh
traffic light

la bicicleta
lah bee-see-KLEH-tah
bicycle

el coche
el KOH-cheh
car

Say the Spanish word aloud.

el coche de policía
el KOH-cheh deh poh-lee-SEE-ah
police car

el camión
el kah-MYOHN
truck

En la playa

la gaviota
lah gah-BYOH-tah
seagull

el pez
el PEHS
fish

la concha
lah KOHN-chah
shell

el mar
el MAHR
sea

At the beach

el alga marina
el AHL-gah mah-REEN-ah
seaweed

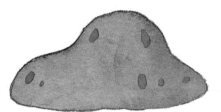

la roca
lah ROH-kah
rock

el velero
el beh-LEH-roh
sailboat

la arena
lah ah-REH-nah
sand

Say the Spanish word aloud.

la ola
lah OH-lah
wave

Mi familia

Look for these words in the big picture.

mi hermano

mee ehr-MAH-noh
brother

mi hermana

mee ehr-MAH-nah
sister

mi padre

mee PAH-dreh
father

mi madre

mee MAH-dreh
mother

How many people are in your family?

My family

mi tío

mee TEE-oh
uncle

mi tía

mee TEE-ah
aunt

mi abuela

mee ah-BWEH-lah
grandmother

mis primos

mees PREE-mohs
cousins

mi abuelo

mee ah-BWEH-loh
grandfather

Say the Spanish word aloud.

19

Una fiesta

Look for these words in the big picture.

el sándwich
el SAHND-weech
sandwich

el helado
el el-AH-doh
ice cream

el pastel
el pahs-TEHL
cake

las papas fritas
lahs PAH-pahs FREE-tahs
french fries

Find some some balloons in another scene.

20

Party time!

el refresco
el reh-FREHS-coh
soda

el jugo de naranja
el HOO-goh deh nah-RAHN-hah
orange juice

el agua
el AH-gwah
water

la pizza
lah PEE-sah
pizza

el chocolate
el choh-koh-LAH-teh
chocolate

Say the Spanish word aloud.

Comprar juguetes

Look for these words in the big picture.

el collar de cuentas
el koh-YAHR deh KWEHN-tahs
beads

el robot
el rroh-BOHT
robot

el rompecabezas
el rrohm-peh-kah-BEH-sahs
jigsaw puzzle

Find a teddy bear in another scene.

el futbolito
el foot-boh-LEE-toh
foosball

Shopping for toys

la pelota
lah peh-LOH-tah
ball

el juego
el HWEH-goh
game

el videojuego
el bee-deh-oh-HWEH-goh
video game

el osito
el oh-SEE-toh
teddy bear

Say the Spanish word aloud.

el avión para armar
el ah-BYOHN PAH-rah ahr-MAHR
model airplane kit

En la cocina

Look for these words in the big picture.

el refrigerador
el reh-free-heh-rah-DOHR
fridge

el vaso
el BAH-soh
glass

la cacerola
lah kah-seh-ROH-lah
saucepan

Find a glass on another page.

el cuchillo
el koo-CHEE-yoh
knife

In the kitchen

el plato
el PLAH-toh
plate

la estufa
lah ehs-TOO-fah
stove

el fregadero
el freh-gah-DEH-roh
sink

Say the Spanish word aloud.

la cuchara
lah koo-CHAH-rah
spoon

el tenedor
el teh-neh-DOHR
fork

En el campo

el árbol
el AHR-bohl
tree

la flor
lah FLOHR
flower

el prado
el PRAH-doh
field

el bosque
el BOHS-keh
forest

In the countryside

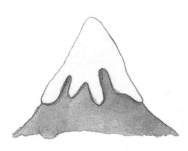

la montaña
lah mohn-TAH-nyah
mountain

la hierba
lah YEHR-bah
grass

el pájaro
el PAH-hah-roh
bird

el puente
el PWEHN-teh
bridge

Say the Spanish word aloud.

el río
el RREE-oh
river

Bañarse

Look for these words in the big picture.

el jabón

el hah-BOHN
soap

el lavabo

el lah-BAH-boh
sink

la ducha

lah DOO-chah
shower

la toalla

lah toh-AH-yah
towel

Find a bathroom on another page in the book.

Getting a bath

el inodoro
el een-oh-DOH-roh
toilet

el espejo
el ehs-PEH-hoh
mirror

el cepillo de dientes
el seh-PEE-yoh deh
DYEHN-tehs
toothbrush

la pasta de dientes
lah PAHS-tah deh DYEHN-tehs
toothpaste

Say the Spanish word aloud.

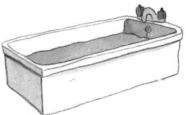

la bañera
lah bah-NYEH-rah
bathtub

En mi dormitorio

Look for these words in the big picture.

la cama
lah KAH-mah
bed

el armario
el ahr-MAH-ryoh
wardrobe

el estante
el ehs-TAHN-teh
shelf

la alfombra
lah ahl-FOHM-brah
rug

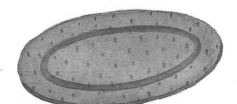

Find a bed in another picture in the book.

30

In my bedroom

la televisión
lah teh-leh-bee-SYOHN
television

la ventana
lah behn-TAH-nah
window

la puerta
lah PWEHR-tah
door

las pantuflas
lahs pahn-TOO-flahs
slippers

el despertador
el dehs-pehr-tah-DOHR
alarm clock

Say the Spanish word aloud.

31

Mi casa

Look for these words in the big picture.

el baño
el BAH-nyoh
toilet

el cuarto de baño
el KWAHR-toh deh BAH-nyoh
bathroom

el techo
el TEH-choh
ceiling

la cocina
lah koh-SEE-nah
kitchen

Find another house in the book.

32

My house

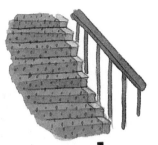

las escaleras
lah ehs-kah-LEH-rahs
stairs

el jardín
el hahr-DEEN
garden

el tejado
el teh-HAH-doh
roof

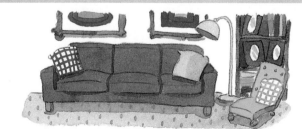

la sala
lah SAH-lah
living room

Say the Spanish word aloud.

el dormitorio
el dohr-mee-TOH-ryoh
bedroom

33

Durante la semana

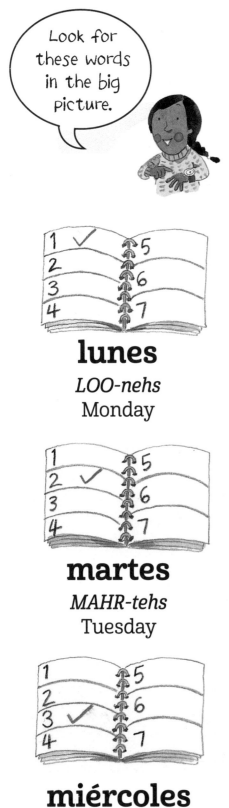

Look for these words in the big picture.

lunes
LOO-nehs
Monday

martes
MAHR-tehs
Tuesday

miércoles
MYEHR-koh-lehs
Wednesday

jueves
HWEH-behs
Thursday

Say the Spanish word aloud.

During the week

What are you doing today?

hoy
OY
today

mañana
mah-NYAH-nah
tomorrow

domingo
doh-MEEN-goh
Sunday

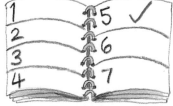

viernes
BYEHR-nehs
Friday

sábado
SAH-bah-doh
Saturday

Visitando a un amigo

Look for these words in the big picture.

hola
OH-lah
hello

no
NOH
no

sí
SEE
yes

por favor
pohr fah-BOHR
please

Say the Spanish word aloud.

Visiting a friend

no es nada
noh ehs NAH-dah
that's okay

adiós
ah-DYOHS
goodbye

gracias
GRAH-syahs
thanks

toma
TOH-mah
here you are

perdón
pehr-DOHN
sorry

En el parque

Look for these words in the big picture.

la niña
lah NEE-nyah
girl

el columpio
el koh-LOOM-pyoh
swing

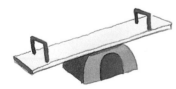

el sube y baja
el SOO-beh ee BAH-hah
seesaw

el camino
el kah-MEE-noh
path

Can you find a swan on another page?

At the park

el niño
el NEE-nyoh
boy

el banco
el BAHN-koh
bench

la cometa
lah koh-MEH-tah
kite

el lago
el LAH-goh
lake

Say the Spanish word aloud.

el niño/la niña
el NEE-nyoh/lah NEE-nyah
child

Hacer deporte

el ping pong

el PEENG-pong
ping pong

esquiar

ehs-KYAHR
skiing

pescar

pehs-KAHR
fishing

el fútbol

el FOOT-bohl
soccer

Playing sports

el atletismo
el aht-leh-TEES-moh
athletics

ir en bicicleta
eer ehn bee-see-KLEH-tah
cycling

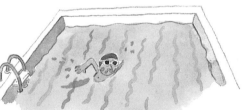

nadar
nah-DAHR
swimming

Say the Spanish word aloud.

la gimnasia
lah heem-NAH-syah
gymnastics

el baloncesto
el bah-lohn-SEHS-toh
basketball

En la ciudad

Look for these words in the big picture.

la casa
lah KAH-sah
house

la estación
lah ehs-tah-SYOHN
station

la escuela
lah ehs-KWEH-lah
school

Find a picture that shows inside a school.

el supermercado
el soo-pehr-mehr-KAH-doh
supermarket

In town

el mercado
el mehr-KAH-doh
market

la tienda
lah TYEHN-dah
store

el cine
el SEE-neh
movie theater

Say the Spanish word aloud.

la fábrica
lah FAH-bree-kah
factory

la oficina de correos
ah oh-feh-SEE-nah deh coh-RREH-ohs
post office

En el supermercado

Look for these words in the big picture.

el huevo
el WEH-boh
egg

la carne
lah KAHR-neh
meat

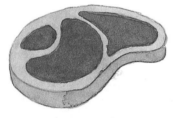

el pan
el PAHN
bread

la mantequilla
lah mahn-teh-KEE-yah
butter

Find milk on another page in the book.

At the supermarket

el arroz
el ah-RROHS
rice

la leche
lah LEH-cheh
milk

el azúcar
el ah-SOO-kahr
sugar

el pescado
el pehs-KAH-doh
fish

Say the Spanish word aloud.

la pasta
la PAHS-tah
pasta

Comprando fruta

Look for these words in the big picture.

la manzana

lah mahn-SAH-nah
apple

el melocotón

el meh-loh-koh-TOHN
peach

la cereza

lah seh-REH-sah
cherry

la piña

lah PEE-nyah
pineapple

Find some fruit in another picture.

Buying fruit

el plátano
el PLAH-tah-noh
banana

las uvas
lahs OO-bahs
grapes

la fresa
lah FREH-sah
strawberry

la naranja
lah nah-RAHN-hah
orange

el mango
el MAHN-goh
mango

Say the Spanish word aloud.

Los opuestos

Look for these words in the big picture.

corto/corta
KOHR-toh/KOHR-tah
short

grande
GRAHN-deh
big

bonito/bonita
boh-NEE-toh/boh-NEE-tah
pretty

pequeño/pequeña
peh-KEH-nyoh/peh-KEH-nyah
small

48

Opposites

feliz
feh-LEES
happy

triste
TREES-teh
sad

bueno/buena
BWEH-noh/BWEH-nah
good

caro/cara
KAH-roh/KAH-rah
expensive

largo/larga
LAHR-goh/gah
long

Say the Spanish word aloud.

¿Qué tiempo hace?

Look for these words in the big picture.

el sol
el SOHL
sun

hace calor
AH-seh kah-LOHR
it's hot

llueve
YWEH-beh
it's raining

Find some rain in another picture.

la nube
lah NOO-beh
cloud

What's the weather like?

el viento
el BYEHN-toh
wind

hace frío
AH-seh FREE-oh
it's cold

nieva
NYEH-bah
it's snowing

la tormenta
lah tohr-MEHN-tah
storm

la niebla
lah NYEH-blah
fog

Say the Spanish word aloud.

Look for these words in the big picture.

marzo

MAHR-soh
March

abril

ah-BREEL
April

mayo

MAH-yoh
May

la estación

la ehs-tah-SYOHN
season

Say the Spanish word aloud.

The year – spring and summer

junio
HOO-nyoh
June

julio
HOO-lyoh
July

agosto
ah-GOHS-toh
August

These months are autumn and winter in the Southern Hemisphere!

la primavera
lah pree-mah-BEH-rah
spring

el verano
el beh-RAH-noh
summer

El año – El otoño y el invierno

Look for these words in the big picture.

9

septiembre
sehp-TYEHM-breh
September

10

octubre
ohk-TOO-breh
October

11

noviembre
noh-BYEHM-breh
November

el otoño
el oh-TOH-nyoh
autumn

Say the Spanish word aloud.

The year – autumn and winter

diciembre
dee-SYEHM-breh
December

enero
eh-NEH-roh
January

febrero
feh-BREH-roh
February

el invierno
el een-BYEHR-noh
winter

el mes
el MEHS
month

These months are spring and summer in the Southern Hemisphere!

Cultivando verduras

la papa
lah PAH-pah
potato

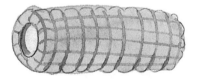

el maíz
el mah-EES
corn

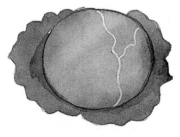

la col
la KOHL
cabbage

la zanahoria
lah sah-nah-OH-ryah
carrot

56

Growing vegetables

el tomate
el toh-MAH-teh
tomato

la lechuga
lah leh-CHOO-gah
lettuce

el apio
el AH-pyoh
celery

el calabacín
el kah-lah-bah-SEEN
cucumber

la berenjena
lah beh-rehn-HEH-nah
eggplant

Find vegetables in another picture in the book.

57

En el bosque

Look for these words in the big picture.

la ardilla
lah ahr-DEE-yah
squirrel

la oruga
lah ohr-OO-gah
caterpillar

el ciervo
el SYEHR-boh
deer

el escarabajo
el ehs-kah-rah-BAH-hoh
beetle

Find a butterfly in another picture.

In the forest

el oso pardo
el OH-so PAHR-doh
brown bear

el conejo
el koh-NEH-hoh
rabbit

la mariposa
lah mah-ree-POH-sah
butterfly

el zorro
el SOH-rroh
fox

la mosca
lah MOH-skah
fly

Say the Spanish word aloud.

59

Las preguntas

¿quién?
KYEHN
who?

¿qué?
KEH
what?

¿cuándo?
KWAHN-doh
when?

¿dónde?
DOHN-deh
where?

Questions

¿cuánto?
KWAHN-toh
how much?

¿cuántos?
KWAHN-tohs
how many?

¿puedo?
PWEH-doh
can I?

¿por qué?
pohr KEH
why?

¿cómo?
KOH-moh
how?

Say the Spanish word aloud.

61

Lista de palabras
LEE-stah deh pah-LAH-brahs

En la granja p. 2 — On the farm
el caballo	horse
la cabra	goat
el cerdo	pig
el gato	cat
la oveja	sheep
el pato	duck
el perro	dog
el ratón	mouse
la vaca	cow

En clase p. 4 — In the classroom
la computadora	computer
el lápiz de color	colored pencil
el libro	book
la mesa	table
el papel	paper
el pegamento	glue
la pluma	pen
la profesora	teacher
la silla	chair

El cuerpo p. 6 — Your body
la boca	mouth
el brazo	arm
la cabeza	head
los hombros	shoulders
la mano	hand
la nariz	nose
los ojos	eyes
el pie	foot
la pierna	leg

Los colores en la selva p. 8 — Colors in the jungle
amarillo/amarilla	yellow
azul	blue
blanco/blanca	white
marrón	brown
morado/morada	purple
naranja	orange
negro/negra	black
rojo/roja	red
verde	green

El baúl de los disfraces p. 10 — The dressing-up box
la ropa	clothes
el abrigo	coat
los calcetines	socks
la camisa	shirt
la falda	skirt
el pantalón	pants
el pijama	pajamas
el sombrero	hat
el vestido	dress
los zapatos	shoes

En el zoológico p. 12 — At the zoo
el cocodrilo	crocodile
el delfín	dolphin
el elefante	elephant
el hipopótamo	hippopotamus
la jirafa	giraffe
el león	lion
el oso polar	polar bear
la víbora	snake
el tigre	tiger

El transporte p. 14 — Transportation
la acera	sidewalk
el autobús	bus
la bicicleta	bicycle
la calle	street
el camión	truck
el coche	car
el coche de policía	police car
la parada	bus stop
el semáforo	traffic light

En la playa p. 16 — At the beach
el alga marina	seaweed
la arena	sand
la concha	shell
la gaviota	seagull
el mar	sea
la ola	wave
el pez	fish
la roca	rock
el velero	sailboat

Mi familia p. 18 — My family
mi abuela	grandmother
mi abuelo	grandfather
mi hermana	sister
mi hermano	brother
mi madre	mother
mi padre	father
mis primos	cousins
mi tía	aunt
mi tío	uncle

Una fiesta p. 20 — Party
el agua	water
el chocolate	chocolate
el helado	ice cream
el jugo de naranja	orange juice
las papas fritas	french fries
el pastel	cake
la pizza	pizza
el refresco	soda
el sándwich	sandwich

Comprar juguetes p. 22 — Shopping for toys
el avión para armar	model airplane kit
el collar de cuentas	beads
el futbolito	foosball
el juego	game
el osito	teddy bear
la pelota	ball
el robot	robot
el rompecabezas	jigsaw puzzle
el videojuego	video game

En la cocina p. 24 — In the kitchen
la cacerola	saucepan
la cuchara	spoon
el cuchillo	knife
la estufa	stove
el fregadero	sink
el plato	plate
el refrigerador	fridge
el tenedor	fork
el vaso	glass

En el campo p. 26 — In the countryside
el árbol	tree
el bosque	forest
la flor	flower
la hierba	grass
la montaña	mountain
el pájaro	bird
el prado	field
el puente	bridge
el río	river

Bañarse p. 28 — Getting a bath
el cuarto de baño	the bathroom
la bañera	bathtub
el cepillo de dientes	toothbrush
la ducha	shower
el espejo	mirror
el inodoro	toilet
el jabón	soap
el lavabo	sink
la pasta de dientes	toothpaste
la toalla	towel

En mi dormitorio p. 30 — In my bedroom
la alfombra	rug
el armario	wardrobe
la cama	bed
el despertador	alarm clock
el dormitorio	the bedroom
el estante	shelf
las pantuflas	slippers
la puerta	door
la televisión	television
la ventana	window

Word list

Mi casa p.32 — My house

el baño	toilet
la cocina	kitchen
el cuarto de baño	bathroom
el dormitorio	bedroom
las escaleras	stairs
el jardín	garden
la sala	living room
el techo	ceiling
el tejado	roof

Days of the Week p.34 — Days of the week

lunes	Monday
martes	Tuesday
miércoles	Wednesday
jueves	Thursday
viernes	Friday
sábado	Saturday
domingo	Sunday
hoy	today
mañana	tomorrow

Visitando a un amigo p.36 — Visiting a friend

adiós	goodbye
gracias	thanks
hola	hello
no	no
no es nada	that's okay
perdón	sorry
por favor	please
sí	yes
toma	here you are

En el parque p.38 — At the park

el banco	bench
el camino	path
el columpio	swing
la cometa	kite
el lago	lake
el niño	boy
el niño/la niña	child
la niña	girl
el sube y baja	seesaw

Hacer deporte p.40 — Playing sports

el atletismo	athletics
el baloncesto	basketball
esquiar	skiing
el fútbol	soccer
la gimnasia	gymnastics
ir en bicicleta	cycling
nadar	swimming
pescar	fishing
el ping pong	ping pong

En la ciudad p.42 — In town

la casa	house
el cine	movie theater
la escuela	school
la estación	station
la fábrica	factory
el mercado	market
la oficina de correos	post office
el supermercado	supermarket
la tienda	store

En el supermercado p.44 — At the supermarket

el arroz	rice
el azúcar	sugar
la carne	meat
el huevo	egg
la leche	milk
la mantequilla	butter
el pan	bread
la pasta	pasta
el pescado	fish

Comprando fruta p.46 — Buying fruit

la cereza	cherry
la fresa	strawberry
el mango	mango
la manzana	apple
el melocotón	peach
la naranja	orange
la piña	pineapple
el plátano	banana
las uvas	grapes

Los opuestos p.48 — Opposites

bonito/bonita	pretty
bueno/buena	good
caro/cara	expensive
corto/corta	short
feliz	happy
grande	big
largo/larga	long
pequeño/pequeña	small
triste	sad

¿Qué tiempo hace? p.50 — What's the weather like?

hace calor	it's hot
hace frío	it's cold
llueve	it's raining
la niebla	fog
nieva	it's snowing
la nube	cloud
el sol	sun
la tormenta	storm
el viento	wind

El año La primavera y el verano p.52 — The year spring and summer

la estación	season
la primavera	spring
marzo	March
abril	April
mayo	May
el verano	summer
junio	June
julio	July
agosto	August

El año El otoño y el invierno p.54 — The year autumn and winter

el otoño	autumn
septiembre	September
octubre	October
noviembre	November
el invierno	winter
diciembre	December
enero	January
febrero	February
el mes	month

Cultivando verduras p.56 — Growing vegetables

el apio	celery
la berenjena	eggplant
el calabacín	cucumber
la col	cabbage
la lechuga	lettuce
el maíz	corn
la papa	potato
el tomate	tomato
la zanahoria	carrot

En el bosque p.58 — In the forest

la ardilla	squirrel
el ciervo	deer
el conejo	rabbit
el escarabajo	beetle
la mariposa	butterfly
la mosca	fly
la oruga	caterpillar
el oso pardo	brown bear
el zorro	fox

Las preguntas p.60 — Questions

¿cómo?	how?
¿cuándo?	when?
¿cuánto?	how much?
¿cuántos?	how many?
¿dónde?	where?
¿por qué?	why?
¿puedo?	can I?
¿qué?	what?
¿quién?	who?

Answers

Page 2
There is another cat on pages 24, 29, and 44.

Page 4
There are other chairs on pages 18, 19, 25, 31, and 32.

Page 6
There are 12 children at the party.

Page 8
There are three purple things in the scene.

Page 10
There is someone wearing a hat on pages 8, 16, 20, 40, 44, 46, 48, 51, 53, 55, 56, 60, and 61.

Page 12
There are other animals that could be in a zoo on pages 8, 55, and 58.

Page 14
There is a car on page 34.

Page 16
There are fish on pages 45 and 46.

Page 20
There are balloons on pages 6 and 7.

Page 22
There is a teddy bear on pages 30 and 33.

Page 24
There are glasses on pages 18, 20, 21, 36, and 37.

Page 26
There are birds on pages 2, 8, 16, 17, 26, 32, 39, 46, and 52.

Page 28
There is a bathroom on page 32.

Page 30
There is a bed on page 32.

Page 32
There is a house on pages 2 and 35.

Page 38
There is a swan on page 27.

Page 40
There are sports being played on pages 34 and 50.

Page 42
There is a picture that shows inside a school on pages 4 and 5.

Page 44
There is milk on page 24.

Page 46
There is fruit on pages 15, 18, and 24.

Page 50
There is rain on pages 52 and 53.

Page 56
There are vegetables on pages 18, 21, and 35.

Page 58
There is a butterfly on pages 8, 9, and 26.

Brief pronunciation notes

Throughout this book, pronunciation guides are included with each word. Here are some general rules to help you get started.

The vowel sounds are approximated this way in the pronunciation guides:
ah is like the short *a* in father
eh is like the short *e* in pet
ee is like the long *ee* sound in cheese
oh is like the long *o* in orange
oo is like the *oo* sound in food

When you see the *rr*, it means to roll or trill the *r* sound in that word. The *d* in the pronunciation is often said more softly, and it can sound more similar to *th* when it is between two vowels.

Seek and Speak Spanish Words © b small publishing ltd.

This edition © 2022 Happy Fox Books, an imprint of Fox Chapel Publishing Company, Inc., 903 Square Street, Mount Joy, PA 17552. First published in 2018 by b small publishing ltd. Spanish advisor, Happy Fox edition: Rosi Perea

Design: Louise Millar
Production: Madeleine Ehm
Language adviser: Diego Blasco Vázquez
Publisher: Sam Hutchinson
Editorial: Sam Hutchinson

Library of Congress Control Number: 2022936156

ISBN 978-1-64124-171-7

We are always looking for talented authors. To submit an idea, please send a brief inquiry to acquisitions@foxchapelpublishing.com.

Printed in China
First printing